COMMUNITY HELPERS

Custodians

by Kate Moening

BLASTOFF! READERS

BELLWETHER MEDIA • MINNEAPOLIS, MN

Note to Librarians, Teachers, and Parents:

Blastoff! Readers are carefully developed by literacy experts and combine standards-based content with developmentally appropriate text.

Level 1 provides the most support through repetition of high-frequency words, light text, predictable sentence patterns, and strong visual support.

Level 2 offers early readers a bit more challenge through varied simple sentences, increased text load, and less repetition of high-frequency words.

Level 3 advances early-fluent readers toward fluency through increased text and concept load, less reliance on visuals, longer sentences, and more literary language.

Level 4 builds reading stamina by providing more text per page, increased use of punctuation, greater variation in sentence patterns, and increasingly challenging vocabulary.

Level 5 encourages children to move from "learning to read" to "reading to learn" by providing even more text, varied writing styles, and less familiar topics.

Whichever book is right for your reader, Blastoff! Readers are the perfect books to build confidence and encourage a love of reading that will last a lifetime!

This edition first published in 2019 by Bellwether Media, Inc.

No part of this publication may be reproduced in whole or in part without written permission of the publisher. For information regarding permission, write to Bellwether Media, Inc., Attention: Permissions Department, 6012 Blue Circle Drive, Minnetonka, MN 55343.

Library of Congress Cataloging-in-Publication Data

LC record for Custodians available at https://lccn.loc.gov/2018030424

Text copyright © 2019 by Bellwether Media, Inc. BLASTOFF! READERS and associated logos are trademarks and/or registered trademarks of Bellwether Media, Inc. SCHOLASTIC, CHILDREN'S PRESS, and associated logos are trademarks and/or registered trademarks of Scholastic Inc., 557 Broadway, New York, NY 10012.

Editor: Betsy Rathburn   Designer: Brittany McIntosh

Printed in the United States of America, North Mankato, MN.

Table of
Contents

Artsy Afternoon

The **students** are making art together. It is fun! But the room gets very messy.

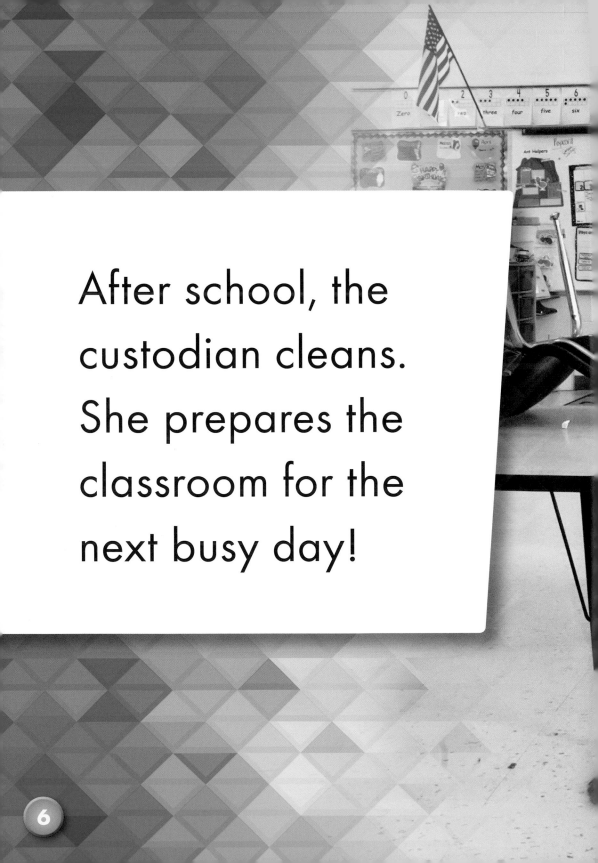

After school, the custodian cleans. She prepares the classroom for the next busy day!

What Are Custodians?

Custodians take care of buildings. They keep spaces clean and safe.

Custodians may work in large buildings. Many work in schools, **hospitals**, or stores.

What Do Custodians Do?

Custodians clean! They mop, wipe, and dust to make rooms feel welcoming.

Some custodians fix machines. If the **air conditioner** breaks, a custodian can help!

air
conditioner

Custodians also take care of building **grounds**. They mow lawns and shovel snow.

Custodian Gear

mop   gloves   tool box   trash can

What Makes a Good Custodian?

Custodians often stand for hours. They must have a lot of **energy**!

CAUTION
WET FLOOR

Custodian Skills

- ✓ good with tools
- ✓ good with details
- ✓ strong
- ✓ energetic

Custodians pay attention to small **details**. They make our world more beautiful!

Glossary

air conditioner

a machine that keeps rooms cool in hot weather

grounds

the area around a building

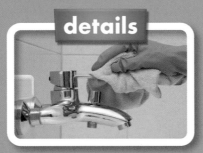

details

small parts that are hard to notice

hospitals

places where people receive emergency care or longer medical visits

energy

the power to work or move

students

people who study, usually in school

To Learn More

AT THE LIBRARY

Bullard, Lisa. *Who Works At Hannah's School?* Minneapolis, Minn.: Millbrook Press, 2018.

Kidde, Rita. *What Does a Janitor Do?* New York, N.Y.: PowerKids Press, 2015.

Manley, Erika S. *Custodians*. Minneapolis, Minn.: Jump!, 2018.

ON THE WEB

FACTSURFER

Factsurfer.com gives you a safe, fun way to find more information.

1. Go to www.factsurfer.com.

2. Enter "custodians" into the search box.

3. Click the "Surf" button and select your book cover to see a list of related web sites.

Index